SHoEs

A POSTCARD BOOK™

TWENTY-EIGHT IMAGES THAT SKIP, STRIDE, AND STRUT THROUGH SHOE HISTORY

RUNNING PRESS

PHILADELPHIA · LONDON

© 1998 by Running Press Book Publishers

All rights reserved under the Pan-American
and International Copyright Conventions

Printed in China

*This book may not be reproduced in whole or in part,
in any form or by any means, electronic or mechanical,
including photocopying, recording, or by any information
storage and retrieval system now known or hereafter
invented, without written permission from the publisher.*

Postcard Book is a trademark of Running Press Book Publishers.

9   8   7   6   5   4   3   2   1
Digit on the right indicates the number of this printing

ISBN 0-7624-0370-5

Designed by Toni Reneé Leslie
Edited by Gena M. Pearson
Photographs © 1998 Kate Swan and Jason Beaupré

This book may be ordered by mail from the publisher.
Please add $2.50 for postage and handling.
But try your bookstore first!

Running Press Book Publishers
125 South Twenty-second Street
Philadelphia, Pennsylvania 19103-4399

Shoes are the quintessential touch of style that make you feel seductive and exciting, funky and hip, or demure and dainty. Just ask Cinderella or Dorothy. Step into the right pair and they'll make you a princess or even carry you home.

As any shoe lover will tell you, the perfect pair are always just a store away. It doesn't matter how many black ones you own, there's always room for another pair. When you slide into them, your whole attitude changes.

Shoes may inspire you to dance 'til dawn or shop 'til you drop. For the shoe lover, there's just no contest between purchasing a pair of shoes or purchasing some other accessory. Shoes will win every time. They evoke fleeting moments like your first date, your senior prom, your successful job interview, the day you met your lover— and the night you dumped him. And, of course, you'll never forget the pair you wore on your wedding day.

Fashion designers the world over have refined a simple invention into a delicious confection for the feet. Now, you'd knock your mother or your best friend down to get a killer-cool pair—or, at the very least, you'd put off paying a bill or two to buy them.

Here, in this beautiful collection, shoes are captured in photographs for you to share with a fellow shoe lover, or to keep and enjoy as a reminder of your eccentric little fetish.

baby needs a new pair of shoes

Heels: a girl's best friend.

little luxuries

STILETTOS • PUMPS • MULES • SANDALS • SLIPPERS • FLATS • SLING-BACKS

PHOTOGRAPH © 1998 KATE SWAN & JASON BEAUPRÉ
Shoes Courtesy of Shoe Museum, Pennsylvania College of Podiatric Medicine
SHOES A POSTCARD BOOK™ © 1998 RUNNING PRESS BOOK PUBLISHERS

Attitude begins at ground level.

true shoe lovers only

STILETTOS • PUMPS • MULES • SANDALS • SLIPPERS • FLATS • SLING-BACKS

PHOTOGRAPH © 1998 KATE SWAN & JASON BEAUPRÉ
SHOES A POSTCARD BOOK™ © 1998 RUNNING PRESS BOOK PUBLISHERS

Looking light on your feet isn't easy.

the lap of luxury

STILETTOS • PUMPS • MULES • SANDALS • SLIPPERS • FLATS • SLING-BACKS

Better that the shoe looks good than feels good.

STILETTOS • PUMPS • MULES • SANDALS • SLIPPERS • FLATS • SLING-BACKS

PHOTOGRAPH © 1998 KATE SWAN & JASON BEAUPRÉ
Shoes Courtesy of Shoe Museum, Pennsylvania College of Podiatric Medicine
SHOES A POSTCARD BOOK™ © 1998 RUNNING PRESS BOOK PUBLISHERS

A shoe without sex appeal is like a flower without petals.

ATTITUDE

STILETTOS • PUMPS • MULES • SANDALS • SLIPPERS • FLATS • SLING-BACKS

PHOTOGRAPH © 1998 KATE SWAN & JASON BEAUPRÉ
SHOES A POSTCARD BOOK™ © 1998 RUNNING PRESS BOOK PUBLISHERS

We never forget the shoes we had on during special
moments of our lives.

**sole
searching**

STILETTOS • PUMPS • MULES • SANDALS • SLIPPERS • FLATS • SLING-BACKS

PHOTOGRAPH © 1998 KATE SWAN & JASON BEAUPRÉ

Shoes Courtesy of Shoe Museum, Pennsylvania College of Podiatric Medicine

SHOES A POSTCARD BOOK™ © 1998 RUNNING PRESS BOOK PUBLISHERS

You can't always change a bad hair style, but you can always change your shoes.

Sleek & Sexy

STILETTOS • PUMPS • MULES • SANDALS • SLIPPERS • FLATS • SLING-BACKS

PHOTOGRAPH © 1998 KATE SWAN & JASON BEAUPRÉ
SHOES A POSTCARD BOOK™ © 1998 RUNNING PRESS BOOK PUBLISHERS

We are what we wear.

decidedly decadent

STILETTOS • PUMPS • MULES • SANDALS • SLIPPERS • FLATS • SLING-BACKS

PHOTOGRAPH © 1998 KATE SWAN & JASON BEAUPRÉ

Shoes Courtesy of Shoe Museum, Pennsylvania College of Podiatric Medicine

SHOES A POSTCARD BOOK™ © 1998 RUNNING PRESS BOOK PUBLISHERS

How tall am I? Honey, with hair, heels, and attitude
I'm through this damned roof!

—RuPaul (b. 1961)
American entertainer

STILETTOS • PUMPS • MULES • SANDALS • SLIPPERS • FLATS • SLING-BACKS

PHOTOGRAPH © 1998 KATE SWAN & JASON BEAUPRÉ
SHOES A POSTCARD BOOK™ © 1998 RUNNING PRESS BOOK PUBLISHERS

The better the slipper, the better the prince.

STILETTOS • PUMPS • MULES • SANDALS • SLIPPERS • FLATS • SLING-BACKS

PHOTOGRAPH © 1998 KATE SWAN & JASON BEAUPRÉ
Shoes Courtesy of Shoe Museum, Pennsylvania College of Podiatric Medicine
SHOES A POSTCARD BOOK™ © 1998 RUNNING PRESS BOOK PUBLISHERS

What cannot be contained must be worn.

STILETTOS • PUMPS • MULES • SANDALS • SLIPPERS • FLATS • SLING-BACKS

A good fit never goes out of style.

Classic

STILETTOS • PUMPS • MULES • SANDALS • SLIPPERS • FLATS • SLING-BACKS

I'll take a look at your slippers. I love them as much
as I do you . . . I breathe their perfume they smell of
verbena.

—Gustave Flaubert (1821–1880)
French writer

STILETTOS • PUMPS • MULES • SANDALS • SLIPPERS • FLATS • SLING-BACKS

PHOTOGRAPH © 1998 KATE SWAN & JASON BEAUPRÉ
SHOES A POSTCARD BOOK™ © 1998 RUNNING PRESS BOOK PUBLISHERS

Shoes are the window to the soul.

the crystal ball of chic

STILETTOS • PUMPS • MULES • SANDALS • SLIPPERS • FLATS • SLING-BACKS

All you have to do is to knock the heels together three times and command the shoes to carry you wherever you wish to go.

—*The Wizard of Oz*
L. Frank Baum (1856–1919)
American writer

STILETTOS • PUMPS • MULES • SANDALS • SLIPPERS • FLATS • SLING-BACKS

PHOTOGRAPH © 1998 KATE SWAN & JASON BEAUPRÉ
Shoes Courtesy the Private Collection of Desire Smith
SHOES A POSTCARD BOOK™ © 1998 RUNNING PRESS BOOK PUBLISHERS

If the shoe fits—buy it!

truly, madly
deeply blue

STILETTOS • PUMPS • MULES • SANDALS • SLIPPERS • FLATS • SLING-BACKS

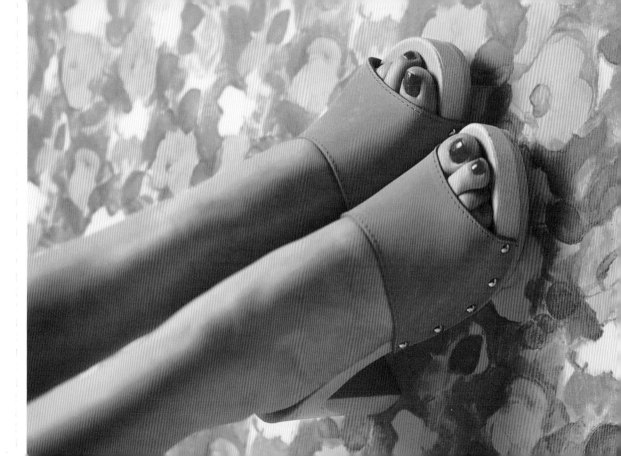

Baby's got a sweet pair of shoes!

STILETTOS • PUMPS • MULES • SANDALS • SLIPPERS • FLATS • SLING-BACKS

No matter how many shoes a woman has, there's always room in her wardrobe for one more pair.

EXCESS

STILETTOS • PUMPS • MULES • SANDALS • SLIPPERS • FLATS • SLING-BACKS

PHOTOGRAPH © 1998 KATE SWAN & JASON BEAUPRÉ
Shoes Courtesy the Private Collection of Desire Smith
SHOES A POSTCARD BOOK™ © 1998 RUNNING PRESS BOOK PUBLISHERS

These shoes were made for walking.

too cool for school

STILETTOS • PUMPS • MULES • SANDALS • SLIPPERS • FLATS • SLING-BACKS

PHOTOGRAPH © 1998 KATE SWAN & JASON BEAUPRÉ
SHOES A POSTCARD BOOK™ © 1998 RUNNING PRESS BOOK PUBLISHERS

Elegance and sophistication—what a wonderful pair!

STILETTOS • PUMPS • MULES • SANDALS • SLIPPERS • FLATS • SLING-BACKS

PHOTOGRAPH © 1998 KATE SWAN & JASON BEAUPRÉ
Shoes Courtesy of Shoe Museum, Pennsylvania College of Podiatric Medicine
SHOES A POSTCARD BOOK™ © 1998 RUNNING PRESS BOOK PUBLISHERS

Never walk a mile in new shoes.

Glamour & Glitz

STILETTOS • PUMPS • MULES • SANDALS • SLIPPERS • FLATS • SLING-BACKS

Angels live above. They do not stand or walk, they glide and sway—floating, laughing, balancing on heels as slender as the stem of a delicate flower.

STILETTOS • PUMPS • MULES • SANDALS • SLIPPERS • FLATS • SLING-BACKS

PHOTOGRAPH © 1998 KATE SWAN & JASON BEAUPRÉ
Shoes Courtesy the Private Collection of Desire Smith
SHOES A POSTCARD BOOK™ © 1998 RUNNING PRESS BOOK PUBLISHERS

All the world's a stage—and the stars get the best shoes.

STILETTOS • PUMPS • MULES • SANDALS • SLIPPERS • FLATS • SLING-BACKS

PHOTOGRAPH © 1998 KATE SWAN & JASON BEAUPRÉ
SHOES A POSTCARD BOOK™ © 1998 RUNNING PRESS BOOK PUBLISHERS

A glimpse of stocking could be shocking.

light
footed

STILETTOS • PUMPS • MULES • SANDALS • SLIPPERS • FLATS • SLING-BACKS

PHOTOGRAPH © 1998 KATE SWAN & JASON BEAUPRÉ
Shoes Courtesy of Shoe Museum, Pennsylvania College of Podiatric Medicine
SHOES A POSTCARD BOOK™ © 1998 RUNNING PRESS BOOK PUBLISHERS

High heels arouse everything from lust to envy to rage.

heeling power

STILETTOS • PUMPS • MULES • SANDALS • SLIPPERS • FLATS • SLING-BACKS

PHOTOGRAPH © 1998 KATE SWAN & JASON BEAUPRÉ
Shoes Courtesy of Shoe Museum, Pennsylvania College of Podiatric Medicine
SHOES A POSTCARD BOOK™ © 1998 RUNNING PRESS BOOK PUBLISHERS

Give a girl the correct footwear and she can
conquer the world.

—Bette Midler (b. 1945)
American singer

STILETTOS • PUMPS • MULES • SANDALS • SLIPPERS • FLATS • SLING-BACKS

The beauty of a shoe lies in the art of wearing it.

avant garde

STILETTOS • PUMPS • MULES • SANDALS • SLIPPERS • FLATS • SLING-BACKS

PHOTOGRAPH © 1998 KATE SWAN & JASON BEAUPRÉ
Shoes Courtesy the Private Collection of Desire Smith
SHOES A POSTCARD BOOK™ © 1998 RUNNING PRESS BOOK PUBLISHERS

It's better to be barefoot than to be caught in the wrong shoes.

obsessed

STILETTOS • PUMPS • MULES • SANDALS • SLIPPERS • FLATS • SLING-BACKS

PHOTOGRAPH © 1998 KATE SWAN & JASON BEAUPRÉ

Shoes Courtesy the Private Collection of Toni Reneé Leslie

SHOES A POSTCARD BOOK™ © 1998 RUNNING PRESS BOOK PUBLISHERS